THE BIG BITE BOOK OF SANDWICHES

THE BIG BITE BOOK OF SANDWICHES

LORNA RHODES

SMITHMARK

This edition published in 1995 by
SMITHMARK Publishers Inc.,
16 East 32nd Street,
New York, NY 10016.

1 2 3 4 5 6 7 8 9

SMITHMARK books are available for bulk purchase
for sales promotion and premium use. For details
write or call the manager of special sales,
SMITHMARK Publishers Inc.,
16 East 32nd Street, New York,
NY 10016; (212) 532-6600

ISBN 0-8317-0983-9

Printed in Singapore

CREDITS

Author and home economist: Lorna Rhodes
Home economist's assistant: Sue Edwards
Managing editor: Lisa Dyer
Photographer: Philip Wilkins
Designers: Paul Johnson and Ian Sandom
Stylist: Marian Price
Filmset: SX Composing Ltd, England
Color Separation: P&W Graphics Pte, Ltd,
    Singapore

Other titles of interest:
The Big Bite Book of BARBECUES
The Big Bite Book of BURGERS
The Big Bite Book of PIZZAS
The Big Bite Book of SALADS

CONTENTS

INTRODUCTION

The Big Bite Book of Sandwiches offers an enticing selection of sandwich recipes to suit all tastes and occasions and to inspire you to create your own unique versions.

The Earl of Sandwich, John Montague, would be amazed to see the kinds of sandwiches we eat today; with exotic ingredients available from all over the world, we have come a long way since 1762 when he invented the sandwich, made up of meat between slices of bread. With the ever-increasing choices of interesting breads, and by using imagination with tasty fillings, sandwiches can be as innovative as you choose.

BREADS

Today it is possible to buy a wide range of bread with different textures, colors and shapes. Pre-sliced forms of white, whole-wheat, multi-grain, rye and pumpernickel are all convenient to use, especially if you need very thin slices for delicate sandwiches. Whole loaves keep fresh longer and can be cut to the thickness appropriate for the sandwich filling, which is deal for open sandwiches that need a substantial base for hearty toppings. Many unusual breads with distinctive flavors, such as ciabatta, focaccia, sourdough and those made with sun-dried tomatoes, olives, nuts and seeds, can now be found in some supermarkets as well as from specialist bakers.

Where a recipe specifies crusty white bread, look for whole loaves, and cut slices from these. Italian and artisan-style bakeries often provide the best quality and range.

In many of the recipes in the book, bread rolls or buns have been used. They are avail-

able in all shapes and sizes and can be soft or crusty. The choice suggested will be appropriate to the filling. For example, a soft filling needs a soft bun, otherwise the filling will squelch out with the first bite. Crusty rolls are more suitable for sliced cold meat and cheese fillings. French baguettes are excellent, but must be eaten the same day as purchased, because they quickly become stale.

Pitas, bagels, English muffins and tortillas can also be used to make sandwiches. Pitas and bagels in particular are available in many different flavors, such as whole-wheat, sesame seed, garlic and onion.

There may be times when there is no bread readily available in your kitchen, so there are a few recipes for quick breads included in the book. With the use of quick-rising dried yeast, a conventional-style loaf is easy to make. Loaves raised with baking powder tend to have a crumbly texture, so they are best eaten with a soft spreadable filling.

SPREADS AND CONDIMENTS

Butter or polyunsaturated margarine are very often used to spread on bread. They will act as a waterproof coating and prevent the filling from making bread slices soggy. Always spread right over the bread to prevent the edges drying. Butter can be made more interesting with the addition of pesto, herbs, garlic, horseradish, mustard and pastes, such as sun-dried

RIGHT: A vast selection of sandwich ingredients can be found in supermarkets, delicatessens and specialty stores. Choose interesting combinations to create your own unique sandwiches.

tomato paste. Mayonnaise has been used in some of the recipes to add moisture to the sandwich and to complement the flavors of the ingredients. Mayonnaise can also have herbs or mustard added for extra flavor. It is also worth looking for a commercial brand of reduced-calorie mayonnaise for a lower-fat spread.

Mustard is an excellent accompaniment to cold meats and there are different strengths, from the milder American and German types to the distinctive Dijon and the grainy varieties which, in particular, complement red meats.

As many of the sandwich recipes use Mediterranean-style breads, the spreads suggested are often based on olives or olive oil. Ready-made tapenades and olive pastes can be bought, but with a food processor it is really easy to make your own. A vast choice of relishes and chutneys are also available from delis and gourmet food stores, and they add interest and taste to sandwiches. For a different spread, try a thin layer of tahini or hummus, which can be topped with cheese, cold meat or fresh salad ingredients.

SANDWICH FILLINGS

There are so many types of sliced meats to use in sandwiches, from simple roasted or poached chicken, cooked beef and boiled ham to cured and smoked meats, that the choices available give plenty of scope for variety. Delicatessens are an excellent source for salamis, pâtés and terrines, as well as cheeses.

Canned fish, such as tuna, salmon and crabmeat, are delicious when mixed with mayonnaise or soft cheese and herbs. Cheeses of all strengths of flavor and texture can be used in sandwiches. Hard cheese can be thinly sliced or grated, some cheese can be crumbled and soft creamy cheese can be spread.

Combine any meats, fish or cheeses with crisp vegetables, such as shredded carrot, celery or iceberg lettuce, and add extra flavor with spreads and condiments.

Remember to keep any prepared sandwiches containing cooked meats, fish, seafood, eggs or cheese in the refrigerator until ready to serve, and consider a chilled method of transporting meat sandwiches if they are not eaten immediately after assembling.

SANDWICHES FOR ALL OCCASIONS

Sandwiches can be eaten at any time of the day as a snack, main meal or for parties or picnics. Some of the recipes in the book are substantial enough for lunch or supper, whereas others are best suited for light luncheons or for hors d'oeuvres.

The picnic ideas in the book also offer a further choice of sandwiches which could provide the main part of an "al fresco" meal. Virtually anything sweet or savory can be transported safely between two slices of bread or in a bun. If you are transporting sandwiches, wrap them well in plastic wrap or wax paper to prevent the bread from becoming stale, and pack the sandwiches in rigid containers to avoid squashing them. An insulated cooler is best for picnics, but look for slim-line ice packs if packing sandwiches in lunchboxes.

For a finishing touch to your packed meal, accompany sandwiches with cherry tomatoes, celery and carrot sticks, or dill pickles and relishes to provide a contrast in flavor and texture to the sandwich.

RIGHT: Colorful and tasty sandwiches really make a memorable picnic, and fresh fruits and vegetables make wonderful accompaniments.

BREADS & CONDIMENTS

Sandwiches can be made more exciting by using interesting breads, and this chapter includes a varied selection of quick and easy bread recipes. The Cornmeal Bread and Quick Carrot Bread are made without yeast and are more crumbly in texture than conventional breads. Homemade relishes, salsas and pastes are sure to add flavor to your sandwiches, and a few recipes are featured here. Most will keep for 3-4 days in the refrigerator, but uncooked herb-based salsas or any made with raw tomatoes, such as Tomato & Herb Salsa, are best used the same day they are prepared.

CORNMEAL BREAD

I cup all-purpose flour
I cup cornmeal
½ teaspoon salt
I teaspoon sugar
2 teaspoons baking powder
2 eggs
I cup milk
2 tablespoons sour cream
4 tablespoons butter, melted

Preheat the oven to 400°F. Mix all the dry ingredients together in a large mixing bowl. Set aside.

In a separate bowl, beat together the eggs, milk, sour cream and butter. Add to the dry cornmeal mixture and stir until just combined. Turn into a shallow, well-greased, 8-inch square baking pan and bake for 18-20 minutes, until the sides pull away from the edge of the pan. Cool in the pan for 5 minutes. Cut the Cornmeal Bread into four squares.

MAKES 4 SQUARES

WALNUT BREAD

3 cups whole-wheat flour
¾ cup rolled oats
I teaspoon salt
¼-ounce package quick-rising dried yeast
I tablespoon dried mixed herbs
¾ cup chopped walnut pieces
1¼ cups warm water
2 tablespoons walnut or olive oil
Cracked wheat, to finish

Place all the dry ingredients, except the cracked wheat, into a large bowl and mix together. Add the warm water and oil, and mix to form a soft dough. Knead the dough on a lightly floured surface for about 5 minutes.

Shape the dough into a smooth ball. Place on a greased baking sheet and flatten slightly. Leave in a warm place to rise for about 30 minutes. Preheat the oven to 425°F.

Brush the top of the loaf with water, sprinkle over the cracked wheat, and bake for 20-25 minutes, or until the loaf sounds hollow when tapped on the bottom. Let cool on a wire rack.   MAKES I LOAF

TOP: Walnut Bread
BOTTOM: Cornmeal Bread

QUICK CARROT BREAD

2 cups finely grated carrot
2½ cups all-purpose flour
2 tablespoons baking powder
1 tablespoon sugar
1 teaspoon salt
1 large egg
4 tablespoons olive oil
¾ cup milk

Preheat the oven to 350°F. Place the grated carrot on layers of paper towel to absorb excess liquid.

Sift the flour with the baking powder in a large bowl. Stir in the sugar and salt. Fold in the carrots and set aside.

In a separate bowl, beat the egg with the oil and milk. Add the egg mixture to the flour mixture and stir to form a batter. Turn into a greased 8½ × 4½-inch loaf pan and bake for about 1 hour, or until a skewer inserted into the middle of the loaf comes out clean. Transfer to a wire rack to cool.

MAKES 1 LOAF

ONION AND ROSEMARY BREAD

Follow the above recipe, omitting the carrot and substituting 2 cups chopped onion, sautéed in 2 tablespoons butter until soft, and 1 teaspoon chopped fresh rosemary.

SUN-DRIED TOMATO ROLLS

1 pound white bread flour
1 teaspoon salt
¼-ounce package quick-rising dried yeast
2 tablespoons finely chopped sun-dried tomatoes
½ cup finely grated cheddar cheese
1¼ cups warm water
2 tablespoons olive oil

Mix the first five ingredients in a large bowl. Add the water and olive oil and mix to form a soft dough. Knead the dough for about 5 minutes on a lightly floured surface. Shape into four rolls, place on a greased baking sheet, and flatten the dough rolls to about ¾ inch in thickness. Leave in a warm place until doubled in size.

Preheat the oven to 425°F. When the rolls have risen, bake them for about 12 minutes until golden. Cool on a wire rack.   MAKES 4-6 ROLLS

TOP: Quick Carrot Bread
BOTTOM: Sun-dried Tomato Rolls

RED PEPPER RELISH

2 tablespoons olive oil
1 small onion, finely chopped
2 cloves garlic, finely chopped
3 cups chopped red bell pepper
⅔ cup vegetable stock
⅔ cup dry white wine
1 tablespoon tomato paste
1 bay leaf
2 teaspoons sugar
Salt and ground black pepper

Heat the olive oil in a saucepan. Add the onion and cook gently for about 8 minutes until golden. Add the chopped garlic and red bell pepper, and cook for about 5 minutes, stirring constantly. Add the stock, white wine, tomato paste, bay leaf and sugar. Simmer uncovered for 20-25 minutes, until thick and chunky. Season with salt and pepper, and let cool.

SERVES 4-6

CORN RELISH

2 cups canned corn kernels
½ red onion, finely chopped
2 stalks celery, finely chopped
1 red bell pepper, cored, seeded and finely diced
1 fresh green chili, seeded and finely chopped
2 cloves garlic, finely chopped
1 tablespoon white wine vinegar
1 tablespoon olive oil

Place the corn kernels in a bowl. Add the remaining ingredients and mix well. Set aside for about 1 hour and stir again to mix before serving.   SERVES 4-6

TOMATO & HERB SALSA

4 plum tomatoes
2 tablespoons finely chopped red onion
1 clove garlic, finely chopped
3 tablespoons finely chopped green bell pepper
2 tablespoons olive oil
2 tablespoons chopped fresh cilantro
1 tablespoon chopped fresh parsley
Salt and ground black pepper

Skin the tomatoes by pouring boiling water over them and leaving for about 30 seconds before draining. Let cool slightly and peel the skins. Scoop out the seeds, cut the tomatoes into small dice, and place in a bowl. Add the remaining ingredients, seasoning with salt and pepper. Mix well, cover with plastic wrap, and refrigerate until required.   SERVES 4

Variation: Add 1-2 fresh green chilies, seeded and finely chopped, for a spicy salsa.

BLACK OLIVE PASTE

1½ cups pitted black olives
1 tablespoon capers
2 canned anchovy fillets
3 tablespoons virgin olive oil
1 small clove garlic, crushed
Pinch of thyme
Pinch of ground bay leaves

If the olives are packed in brine, rinse them in cold water. Rinse the capers in water and drain. Place all the ingredients in a food processor and blend until very finely chopped and almost a paste in consistency. Use instead of butter in sandwiches.   SERVES 4-6

CLOCKWISE: Corn Relish, Tomato & Herb Salsa, Black Olive Paste, Red Pepper Relish

LIGHT SELECTIONS

The sandwich recipes in this chapter are suitable for all occasions when light but tasty snacks are required. Along with Mediterranean-style open-faced toasts and lightly filled sandwiches for snacks or lunch-time meals, there are delicate egg and cucumber sandwiches for afternoon teas and novel hors d'oeuvres and appetizers, such as Nutty Cheese Puffs and Crab Melts. Some, like the Blue Cheese & Ham Finger Sandwiches, are ideal for serving at cocktail parties. In addition, many of the sandwich recipes include flavored butters which can be used in your own inspired creations.

HAM SALAD SANDWICHES

8 slices whole-wheat bread
8 ounces thinly sliced ham
1 cup grated cheddar or Double Gloucester cheese
2 tomatoes, sliced
1 pint container cress sprouts, trimmed and washed

TOMATO BUTTER

6 tablespoons butter, softened
2 teaspoons tomato paste
Squeeze lemon juice
Salt and ground black pepper

Prepare the Tomato Butter. Mix the butter, tomato paste, lemon juice and salt and pepper in a bowl until well blended. Spread over all the slices of bread.

Divide the ham between four slices of bread, and add a layer of cheese and a layer of tomato. Top each sandwich with cress. Cover with the remaining bread, butter sides down. Cut each sandwich into quarters and serve.
SERVES 4

HERBY EGG SALAD SANDWICHES

6 hard-boiled eggs, shelled
3 tablespoons mayonnaise
2 tablespoons chopped fresh dill
2 tablespoons chopped fresh chives
8 slices white sandwich bread
Salt and ground black pepper

WATERCRESS BUTTER

4 tablespoons butter, softened
3 tablespoons finely chopped watercress
1 tablespoon chopped fresh parsley

Finely chop the eggs. Place the egg in a bowl, with the mayonnaise, dill and chives. Season with salt and pepper, and fold the mixture together to combine. Refrigerate until required.

Prepare the Watercress Butter. Mix the butter, watercress and parsley together in a bowl until well blended. Spread the butter over all the slices of bread.

Top four slices of the buttered bread with the reserved egg mixture. Cover with the remaining bread, butter sides down. Cut the sandwiches into triangles and serve.
SERVES 4

RIGHT: Ham Salad Sandwiches,
Herby Egg Salad Sandwiches

CURRIED CHICKEN SALAD SANDWICHES

8 ounces cooked chicken, shredded
2 tablespoons chopped fresh cilantro
Lettuce leaves
20 slices cucumber
8 slices brown sandwich bread, lightly buttered
7-ounce can peach slices, drained

CURRIED MAYONNAISE

4 tablespoons mayonnaise
2 teaspooons curry paste
1 tablespoon mango or other fruity chutney

Prepare the Curried Mayonnaise. Mix the mayonnaise and curry paste in a small bowl until well blended. Stir in the chutney.

Fold the shredded chicken and chopped cilantro into the mayonnaise.

Place a layer of lettuce leaves over four slices of bread and top with a layer of cucumber. Divide the chicken mixture between the sandwiches.

Cut the peach slices in half lengthwise and arrange in layers over the chicken mixture. Cover with the remaining bread, cut the sandwiches into quarters, and serve at once. SERVES 4

LIVERWURST DELIGHT SANDWICHES

1 small red bell pepper
1 small green bell pepper
1 small yellow bell pepper
8 ounces smooth liverwurst
12 slices thinly-cut white bread, lightly buttered
1 red onion, thinly sliced
4 tablespoons German mustard

Core and seed the bell peppers. Chop them into small dice and mix the colors together in a bowl. Set aside.

Spread half the liverwurst over four slices of buttered bread. Divide the onion between them. Cover each with a slice of buttered bread, butter side down, and spread the mustard over the top of the bread slices. Scatter the mixed-colored diced bell pepper over the mustard.

Spread the remaining liverwurst over the remaining bread slices. Place on top of the peppers, liverwurst sides down. Press down gently and cut each sandwich into quarters, making small, square, layered sandwiches. Serve at once. SERVES 4

Variation: Substitute liver pâté for the liverwurst in this recipe.

RIGHT: Curried Chicken Salad Sandwich

PROSCIUTTO & CHEESE TOASTS

8 slices Italian bread, such as ciabatta
Extra virgin olive oil
2 cloves garlic, halved
8 ounces Taleggio or Fontina cheese,
rind removed
8 slices prosciutto
2 tomatoes, sliced
Fresh basil sprigs, to garnish

Preheat a broiler to hot. Brush the bread with the olive oil and toast under the broiler until golden on both sides.

Rub the cut sides of the garlic over the toasted bread. Slice the cheese and divide between the toasted bread. Top each toast with a slice of prosciutto, arranging it in folds. Halve the tomato slices and place in the folds of the prosciutto. Garnish with basil sprigs and serve at once, serving two slices to each person. SERVES 4

MUSHROOM TOASTS

12 slices French bread, each about
¼ inch thick
2 tablespoons butter
2 tablespoons olive oil
2 cloves garlic, thinly sliced
3 cups sliced cultivated mushrooms
8 ounces whole wild mushrooms, such as
chanterelles or girolles
2 tablespoons chopped fresh parsley
Salt and ground black pepper

Preheat a broiler to hot and toast the bread slices under the broiler until golden on both sides.

Meanwhile, melt the butter in a skillet and add the oil and garlic. After 30 seconds, stir in the culti-

vated mushrooms. Cook over a high heat for 3 minutes, tossing them in the skillet the whole time. Add the wild mushrooms and cook for a further 2 minutes. Stir in the parsley and season with salt and pepper. Spoon onto the toasted bread and serve three toasts to each person while still hot. SERVES 4

TUSCAN-STYLE TOASTS

8 slices sciocco or Italian flat bread
2 tomatoes, cut into small wedges

ARUGULA PESTO
About 1 ounce arugula leaves
1 clove garlic, crushed
3 tablespoons pine nuts, lightly toasted
2 tablespoons grated Parmesan cheese
2 tablespoons virgin olive oil
Salt and ground black pepper

Preheat a broiler to hot. Prepare the pesto. Place the arugula and garlic in a food processor and chop finely. Add 2 tablespoons of the pine nuts and blend again until very finely chopped. Add the Parmesan and, with the processor running, add the oil gradually until the mixture becomes smooth. Season with salt and pepper. Set aside.

Toast the bread under the broiler until golden on both sides. Spread the Arugula Pesto over the toasted bread. Arrange wedges of tomato on top of each, then scatter the remaining pine nuts on top. Serve two toasts to each person. SERVES 4

TOP TO BOTTOM: Prosciutto & Cheese Toasts, Mushroom Toasts, Tuscan-Style Toasts

GRILLED HAM & CHEESE SANDWICHES

8 slices white bread
½ cup butter
8 thin slices Gruyère or cheddar cheese
4 slices ham
Ground black pepper
6 tablespoons sunflower oil

Butter all the bread slices. Place a slice of cheese on each of four buttered slices. Top each with a slice of ham, season with black pepper and top with another slice of cheese. Finish with the remaining bread slices, butter sides down, to make four sandwiches. Press down firmly.

Melt half the remaining butter in a large skillet with half the sunflower oil. Fry two sandwiches until golden brown and crisp, turning once. Cook the other two sandwiches in the same way, using the remaining butter and oil. Serve while still hot.   SERVES 4

GRILLED PEPPERONI SANDWICHES

8 slices white bread
½ cup butter
9 ounces mozzarella cheese, thinly sliced
1 cup sliced pepperoni
2 tomatoes, thinly sliced
Ground black pepper
6 tablespoons sunflower oil

Butter all the bread. Arrange half the cheese over four slices of bread and divide the pepperoni between them. Add the tomato slices, season with pepper, and finish with the remaining cheese. Cover with the remaining bread and press down. Follow the instructions for Grilled Ham and Cheese Sandwiches, above, to cook the sandwiches.   SERVES 4

NUTTY CHEESE PUFFS

4 thick slices white bread
½ cup finely grated cheddar cheese
1 tablespoon finely chopped onion
2 tablespoons mayonnaise
1 tablespoon chopped fresh parsley
¼ cup chopped pecans
1 egg, separated
Mixed lettuce leaves, to serve (optional)

Preheat a broiler to hot. Using a 2-inch round biscuit cutter, cut three circles from each slice of bread. Place under the broiler and toast until golden on both sides. Set aside. Preheat the oven to 350°F.

Place the cheese, onion, mayonnaise, parsley, nuts and egg yolk into a bowl and mix until combined. In a separate bowl, whisk the egg white until stiff. Fold the egg white into the cheese mixture. Divide between the rounds of toast and place on a baking sheet. Bake for 8-10 minutes.

Serve three cheese puffs to each person while still hot, along with a few lettuce leaves if desired.
SERVES 4

RIGHT: Nutty Cheese Puffs

BLUE CHEESE & HAM FINGER SANDWICHES

4 ounces Roquefort cheese, rind removed
2 tablespoons crème fraîche
I cup finely chopped ham
6 slices thinly-cut whole-wheat bread

Place the Roquefort in a bowl and break into small pieces. Add the crème fraîche and beat together to mix well. Fold in the chopped ham. Spread the mixture on three slices of bread, cover with the remaining bread, and trim off the crusts.

Cut each sandwich in half lengthwise, then across four times to make each into eight small sandwiches. Serve as an hors d'oeuvre or for a snack. SERVES 4

ENGLISH CUCUMBER SANDWICHES

I cucumber, peeled and thinly sliced
½ teaspoon salt
4 tablespoons butter, softened
2 tablespoons chopped fresh herbs, such as parsley, chervil and dill
¼ teaspoon Dijon mustard
8 thin slices white bread
2 tablespoons chopped fresh mint

Place the cucumber in a colander and sprinkle with salt. Leave for 30 minutes to draw excess moisture from the cucumber. Pat dry with paper towels.

Beat the butter with the herbs and mustard, and use it to butter all the bread slices.

Arrange the cucumber slices over four slices of buttered bread. Scatter over the mint and cover with the remaining bread. Press the sandwiches together.

Carefully trim the crusts and cut each sandwich into four squares. Cut each square in half diagonally to make two dainty triangles. SERVES 4

CREAM CHEESE PINWHEELS

3 large slices white bread
3 large slices brown bread
8 ounces soft cream cheese
2 tablespoons sour cream or crème fraîche
I cup finely chopped smoked salmon
2 tablespoons chopped fresh dill
Squeeze lemon juice
Ground black pepper
Fresh dill sprigs, to garnish

Remove the crusts from the bread. Place each on a work surface and flatten with a rolling pin.

Beat the cream cheese and sour cream together in a bowl. Stir in the smoked salmon, dill, lemon juice and a little black pepper. Spread the mixture over all the bread slices. Roll up each slice from the short end to enclose the filling. Wrap each roll in plastic wrap and refrigerate for at least 1 hour.

To serve, remove the plastic wrap and cut each roll into ¾-inch wide slices. Arrange on a serving platter, garnish with dill sprigs, and serve as an hors d'oeuvre or a tea-time treat. SERVES 4

Variation: Omit the smoked salmon for a simple herby version, or substitute ½ cup chopped ham for the smoked salmon.

RIGHT: English Cucumber Sandwiches, Blue Cheese & Ham Finger Sandwiches, Cream Cheese Pinwheels

CRAB MELTS

1½ cups fresh or canned crabmeat
2 tablespoons fromage blanc or crème fraîche
2 teaspoons lemon juice
2 teaspoons tomato ketchup
2 teaspoons chopped fresh parsley
Salt and ground black pepper
2 English muffins
2 teaspoons grated Parmesan cheese
Lemon twists, to garnish (optional)

If using canned crabmeat, drain any excess water in which it is packed. Place the crabmeat in a bowl and break up any large pieces with a fork. In a separate bowl, mix together the fromage blanc, lemon juice, ketchup and parsley. Season with a little salt and pepper, and fold the mixture into the crabmeat. Preheat a broiler to hot.

Split the English muffins and toast them under the broiler. Divide the crab mixture between each muffin half and scatter the Parmesan on top. Return the muffins to the broiler and cook until the top is golden and the crab is heated through. Cut each muffin half into four and serve four pieces to each person while still hot. Garnish with lemon twists, if desired. SERVES 4

Variation: Substitute drained canned tuna for the crabmeat in the recipe to make Tuna Melts, and serve the muffin halves either whole for a lunch-time meal or cut into pieces for an hors d'oeuvre.

LEMONY SHRIMP SALAD ROLLS

8 miniature bread rolls, assorted flavors
3 tablespoons thick mayonnaise
1 teaspoon grated lemon zest
2 teaspoons lemon juice
Ground black pepper
1 tablespoon chopped fresh chives
6 ounces peeled, cooked shrimp

Cut the tops off the bread rolls and hollow out the middle of the bottom halves. Place the mayonnaise in a bowl and mix in the lemon zest, lemon juice, a little black pepper and the chopped chives. Set aside.

Reserve eight whole shrimp for a garnish. Chop the remaining shrimp and fold them into the prepared mayonnaise. Spoon some of the shrimp mixture into each bread roll. Replace the bread lids and secure with wooden skewers. Garnish each sandwich with a whole shrimp and serve two sandwiches to each person.

SERVES 4

RIGHT: Crab Melts, Lemony Shrimp Salad Rolls

FLORENTINE SANDWICHES

2 ounces young spinach leaves, washed and dried
3 slices bacon
1 small red onion, finely sliced
A little butter, softened
8 slices crusty white bread
4 tomatoes, sliced

DRESSING

2 tablespoons extra virgin olive oil
1 teaspoon sugar
2 teaspoons white wine vinegar
2 teaspoons Worcestershire sauce

Preheat a broiler to hot. Place the spinach leaves in a bowl. Whisk all the dressing ingredients together in a separate bowl. Set aside.

Cook the bacon under the broiler until crisp. Drain on paper towels. Crumble the bacon and add it to the spinach. Add the onion slices and dressing to the spinach and toss together well to combine.

Butter four slices of bread. Divide the tomato slices between the bread and top with the spinach mixture. Cover with the remaining bread to make four sandwiches, cut each in half, and serve.   SERVES 4

Variation: For a heartier sandwich, place a fried egg on top of the spinach in each sandwich.

TUNA & OLIVE SANDWICHES

1 small red bell pepper
7-ounce can tuna, drained
¾ cup pitted green olives, sliced
1 tablespoon chopped capers or
2 tablespoons diced dill pickle
1 tablespoon crème fraîche
2 tablespoons mayonnaise
A little butter, softened
8 slices soft mixed-grain bread
Lettuce leaves

Preheat a broiler to hot. Roast the red bell pepper by placing it under the hot broiler and turning occasionally until it is charred all over. Remove from the broiler and place in a plastic bag. Set aside for 20 minutes. Peel off the skin, discard the seeds, and chop the flesh into small dice. Set aside.

Place the tuna in a bowl and flake with a fork to break up large pieces. Add the diced roast bell pepper, sliced olives and chopped capers. In a separate bowl, blend together the crème fraîche and the mayonnaise, and fold into the tuna mixture.

Butter four slices of the bread and arrange lettuce leaves on top. Spoon one-quarter of the tuna filling over each sandwich. Cover with the remaining bread, cut each sandwich in half, and serve.   SERVES 4

RIGHT: Tuna & Olive Sandwich

HEALTHY SANDWICHES

Fresh vegetables, fruits, beans and cheeses are ingredients that feature predominantly in the recipes in this chapter. Although the emphasis is on vegetarian-style sandwiches, the Niçoise Rolls include tuna and the Chicken Waldorf Sandwiches are made with gently poached chicken breast. Many of the recipes use raw vegetables and nutty breads, but for a completely fruit-based sandwich try the Tropical Salad Bowl Sandwich, made with mango, kiwi, pineapple and muesli bread.

GARDEN VEGETABLE SANDWICHES

3 tablespoons olive oil
3 cloves garlic, finely chopped
2 cups sliced broccoli florets
Salt and ground black pepper
I long Italian-style basil bread loaf or ciabatta loaf
2 plum tomatoes, sliced
Fresh basil sprigs, to garnish

Preheat the oven to 350°F. Heat the oil in a skillet and add the garlic. After 30 seconds, add the broccoli and stir-fry for 2 minutes. Add 5 tablespoons of water, cover, and cook for 4-5 minutes, until the broccoli is just tender. Drain any excess water, then set aside to cool. When cool, season with salt and pepper to taste.

Place the bread in the oven to warm as directed on the wrapper, or for 5 minutes.

Cut the loaf lengthwise and arrange the tomatoes on the base. Season and place the broccoli on top. Cut the loaf into four portions, garnish with basil, and serve while the bread is still warm.   SERVES 4

MUSHROOM & PEPPER SANDWICHES

2 tablespoons olive oil
3 cups roughly chopped mushrooms
I clove garlic
I red bell pepper, cored, seeded and roughly chopped
½ teaspoon dried thyme
¼ teaspoon cayenne pepper
¼ cup shelled sunflower seeds
Salt and ground black pepper
8 slices Spanish-style seeded bread
Crisp lettuce leaves

Heat the olive oil in a skillet. Add the mushrooms, garlic, red bell pepper, thyme and cayenne pepper. Cook over a high heat for 5 minutes until the mushrooms soften. Let cool.

Transfer the mixture to a food processor. Add the sunflower seeds and blend until the ingredients are finely chopped. Season with salt and pepper.

Spread the mushroom mixture over four bread slices. Place a layer of crisp lettuce leaves on top of each sandwich. Cover with the remaining bread slices and serve.   SERVES 4

TOP: Garden Vegetable Sandwich
BOTTOM: Mushroom & Pepper Sandwich

SPROUT SANDWICHES

I cup small broccoli florets
1½ cups bean sprouts, such as alfalfa or mung bean,
rinsed and drained
4 scallions, chopped
½ cup finely shredded snow peas
4 large pita breads

DRESSING

I tablespoon sunflower oil
I teaspoon dark soy sauce
I teaspoon chili sauce
I tablespoon sesame seeds

Place the broccoli in a small pan with boiling water and cook for 2 minutes. Drain, rinse under cold water, and drain again. Wrap the broccoli in paper towels to absorb any excess water. Transfer to a bowl and add the bean sprouts, scallions and snow peas.

Mix all the dressing ingredients together in a small bowl. Add the dressing to the vegetables and toss together well.

Cut each pita bread in half and open to make pockets (this is often easier if the pitas are warmed first). Fill each pita with one-quarter of the dressed vegetables and serve.   SERVES 4

CRUNCHY HEALTH SANDWICHES

You will find it easiest to use a food processor to shred and slice the vegetables in this recipe.

2 cups shredded radishes
I cup shredded white cabbage
2 stalks celery, finely sliced
½ cup roughly chopped pecans
8 slices mixed-grain bread
Extra pecans, to serve (optional)

DRESSING

3 tablespoons reduced-calorie mayonnaise
3 tablespoons Greek yogurt
I tablespoon lemon juice
2 teaspoons honey
Salt and ground black pepper

Place the radish, cabbage, celery and pecans in a bowl and toss together well.

Whisk all the dressing ingredients together in a small bowl until smooth and thoroughly combined. Stir the dressing into the raw salad ingredients. Divide the salad between four slices of bread. Press down lightly and top with the remaining slices of bread. Cut each sandwich in half and serve with extra pecans, if desired.   SERVES 4

RIGHT: Crunchy Health Sandwich

CHEESE & TOMATO PESTO SANDWICHES

8 large slices or 16 small slices mixed-grain bread
6 ounces Edam cheese, sliced
2 beefsteak tomatoes, sliced
Salt and ground black pepper

TOMATO PESTO

8 oil-packed sun-dried tomatoes
4 tablespoons fresh parsley sprigs
2 shallots, coarsely chopped
1 clove garlic
1 teaspoon balsamic vinegar
2 tablespoons oil from the sun-dried tomatoes

Prepare the pesto. Place all the pesto ingredients into a food processor and blend until very finely chopped.

Spread the Tomato Pesto on four large slices of bread or eight small slices. Arrange cheese slices on top of each sandwich. Top each with tomato slices, and season with salt and pepper. Cover with the remaining bread. Serve one large sandwich or two small sandwiches to each person.   SERVES 4

AVOCADO SANDWICHES

1 large avocado
3 ounces low-fat soft cheese with herbs
Ground black pepper
Quick Carrot Bread (see page 12)
1 small Vidalia onion, sliced
2 tablespoons chopped fresh parsley or chervil
A little polyunsaturated margarine, softened

Halve the avocado, discard the pit, and scoop the flesh into a bowl. Mash with a fork to break it up, but leave small pieces. Mix in the soft cheese and season with black pepper.

Cut 12 slices from the carrot loaf. Spread the avocado mixture over six slices and top with a layer of onion. Scatter the parsley or chervil over the top.

Spread the remaining slices of carrot bread with margarine, place on top of the sandwiches, margarine sides down, and cut each in half. Serve three halves to each person.   SERVES 4

TOP: Avocado Sandwich
BOTTOM: Cheese & Tomato Pesto Sandwich

VEGETARIAN CLUBS

4 ounces young spinach leaves, washed

1½ cups cashews

5 tablespoons Greek yogurt or crème fraîche

Salt and ground black pepper

2 large carrots, peeled

6 scallions, thinly sliced

2 teaspoons poppyseeds

1 tablespoon extra virgin olive oil

2 teaspoons lemon juice

A little butter or polyunsaturated margarine, softened

12 slices mixed-grain bread

Roughly shred the spinach leaves. Place the spinach in a saucepan with just the water that clings to the leaves and cook over a medium heat, stirring for 2 minutes or until wilted. Drain any excess water and let cool. Preheat a broiler to hot.

Place the cashews on a baking sheet and toast under the hot broiler until golden. Let cool. Transfer the nuts to a food processor and blend until finely chopped. Mix the nuts, spinach and yogurt together in a bowl. Season with salt and pepper, and set aside.

With a vegetable peeler, shave thin ribbons of carrot down the length of each carrot, discarding the inner core of each carrot. Place in a bowl and add the scallions and poppyseeds. Sprinkle the olive oil and lemon juice over, and toss to mix well. Set aside.

Butter four slices of bread. Top each with one-quarter of the spinach and nut mixture. Spread another four slices of bread with butter and place over the sandwiches, butter sides up. Divide the carrot mixture between the portions and cover with the remaining bread. Cut each sandwich into four triangles, and serve at once.   SERVES 4

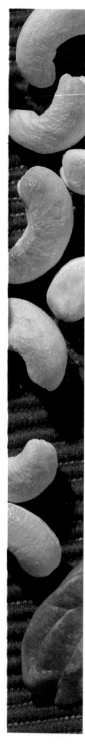

MOSAIC SANDWICHES

The white, green and orange colors of the ingredients make beautiful sandwiches that are healthy and tasty, too.

Walnut Bread (see page 10)

1 cup cottage cheese

1 bunch watercress or arugula, trimmed and chopped

2 clementines, satsumas or tangerines

Ground black pepper

Place the cottage cheese and watercress or arugula in a large mixing bowl. Peel the clementines, removing all the white pith, and cut in between the membranes to produce sections. Chop the fruit sections into small pieces and add to the cottage cheese. Mix all the ingredients together to combine well.

Cut eight slices of bread from the loaf. Divide the filling between four of the slices and top with the remaining bread. Cut each sandwich in half to serve.

SERVES 4

RIGHT: Vegetarian Club

ZESTY BEAN PITAS

2 tablespoons olive oil

1 small onion, finely chopped

2 cups diced parsnips

1 fresh green chili, seeded and finely chopped

2 cloves garlic, finely chopped

1 teaspoon garam masala

½ teaspoon ground cumin

1 teaspoon lemon juice

15-ounce can lima beans, drained

Salt and ground black pepper

2 tablespoons chopped fresh cilantro

3 tomatoes, sliced

4 pita breads, split lengthwise

Extra olive oil (optional)

Heat the oil in a skillet. Add the onion and parsnips and cook gently for 8-10 minutes, until the parsnips begin to soften. Add the chili, garlic and spices, and cook for a further 2 minutes. Cool slightly.

Transfer the mixture to a food processor, along with the lemon juice and lima beans. Process until the ingredients are finely chopped and soft, but before the mixture becomes a paste. Season with salt and pepper, and stir in the cilantro.

To serve, layer the tomato slices in each pita and top with the bean spread. Drizzle in a little extra olive oil, if desired, and serve.　　　　SERVES 4

Variation: Substitute eight slices of country-style bread for the pitas and layer the bean spread on four slices. Top with the tomatoes, a little olive oil, and the remaining bread slices.

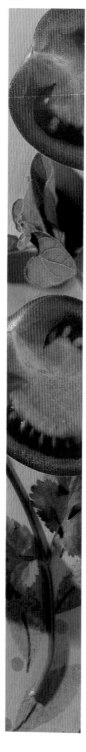

FETA & TOMATO PITAS

4 radicchio leaves, shredded

6 Romaine lettuce leaves, shredded

1½ cups diced feta cheese

4-inch piece cucumber, diced

4 plum tomatoes, diced

12 radishes, sliced

8 black olives, pitted and chopped

4 individual pita breads

Small onion slices, to garnish (optional)

DRESSING

2 tablespoons olive oil

1 tablespoon lemon juice

1 teaspoon dried oregano

1 clove garlic, finely chopped

Salt and ground black pepper

Place the prepared radicchio, lettuce, feta, cucumber, tomato, radish and olives in a large bowl.

Whisk all the dressing ingredients together in a small bowl until thoroughly combined. Stir into the prepared salad ingredients and toss gently together.

Cut open the pita breads to make pockets and spoon one-quarter of the filling into each one. Serve garnished with onion slices, if desired.　　SERVES 4

TOP: Feta & Tomato Pitas
BOTTOM: Zesty Bean Pita

CHICKEN WALDORF SANDWICHES

3 skinless, boneless chicken breasts
⅔ cup chicken stock
4 tablespoons dry white wine
2 tablespoons Greek yogurt
2 tablespoons reduced-calorie mayonnaise
2 tablespoons chopped fresh mint
1 cup halved green or red seedless grapes
3 stalks celery, sliced
A little butter, softened
8 slices French or Italian country-style bread
Lollo rosso or oak leaf lettuce

Place the chicken breasts in a large skillet, pour over the stock and wine, and slowly bring to a simmer. Cover and poach the chicken for about 15 minutes, until the chicken is tender. Let cool in the liquid, then lift the chicken from the skillet and set aside.

Bring the remaining liquid to a boil and boil rapidly until reduced to 3 tablespoons. Pour the liquid into a bowl and let cool. When cool, whisk in the yogurt, mayonnaise and mint. Place the grapes and celery in a separate bowl and fold in the yogurt mixture.

Lightly butter four of the bread slices and arrange a layer of lettuce leaves on top of each. Slice the reserved chicken and place over the lettuce. Top with the celery and grape mixture. Cover with the remaining bread slices, cut each sandwich in half, and serve.

SERVES 4

TROPICAL SALAD BOWL SANDWICHES

The meusli bread combines well with the fruit in this recipe, but for a lower-calorie sandwich you may like to substitute a light diet bread.

1 mango
2 kiwis
2 rings canned pineapple
3 tablespoons Greek yogurt
2-inch piece fresh ginger root, peeled
A little butter or polyunsaturated margarine, softened
8 slices meusli bread with fruit and nuts
Shredded lettuce
Tropical dried fruit and nut trail mix, to serve (optional)

Peel the mango and kiwis, and cut into thin slices. Chop the pineapple into chunks. Set aside.

Place the yogurt in a bowl. Cut the ginger root into manageable pieces and squeeze through a garlic press into the bowl. Let the juice and purée from the ginger mix into the yogurt and stir well to combine. Set aside.

Lightly butter the slices of bread and top four slices with some shredded lettuce. Arrange the mango and kiwi slices on top of each, and scatter over the pineapple. Spoon on the gingered yogurt and top with the remaining bread. Serve with the tropical fruit and nut trail mix, if desired.

SERVES 4

RIGHT: Tropical Salad Bowl Sandwich

NICOISE ROLLS

7-ounce can tuna in water, drained
I cup diced, cooked new potatoes
½ cup cooked thin green beans, cut into
short lengths
4 scallions, chopped
3 tablespoons reduced-calorie mayonnaise
I tablespoon lemon juice
4 olive rolls or individual French baguettes
3 tablespoons Black Olive Paste (see page 14) or
sun-dried tomato paste
4 hard-boiled eggs, shelled and sliced
½ bunch watercress, washed and trimmed
2 tomatoes, sliced
Salt and ground black pepper
2 tablespoons extra virgin olive oil

Flake the tuna in a bowl and add the potato, green beans and scallion. In a separate bowl, mix the mayonnaise and lemon juice together. Stir the mayonnaise into the tuna mixture and set aside.

Cut the rolls or baguettes in half lengthwise and remove some of the soft bread from the inside base to make a hollow in each half. Spread each base with olive or sun-dried tomato paste and arrange sliced egg along the length, followed by sprigs of watercress. Top with the tuna mixture and slices of tomato.

Season with salt and pepper, and drizzle a little olive oil over each sandwich. Cover with the bread lids and serve at once.   SERVES 4

ARUGULA & PARMESAN ROLLS

2 ounces arugula leaves, washed and dried
I cup sliced mushrooms
2-ounce piece Parmesan cheese
4 Sun-dried Tomato Rolls (see page 12)

DRESSING
3 tablespoons extra virgin olive oil
2 teaspoons balsamic vinegar
I clove garlic, finely chopped
½ teaspoon Dijon mustard
Salt and ground black pepper

Place the arugula leaves and mushrooms in a bowl. Whisk all the dressing ingredients together in a separate bowl, seasoning with salt and pepper to taste. Stir the dressing into the arugula salad and toss together well to coat the leaves and mushrooms.

Using a vegetable peeler, shave the Parmesan cheese into flakes.

Cut the rolls horizontally and divide the dressed arugula salad between them. Top each sandwich with the Parmesan flakes and serve.   SERVES 4

TOP: Arugula & Parmesan Rolls
BOTTOM: Niçoise Roll

ROAST VEGETABLE SANDWICHES

2 whole bulbs garlic
Olive oil
3 small beets
2 medium carrots, peeled
2 medium zucchini
2 small red onions, thickly sliced
8 slices sunflower or mixed-grain bread
Salt and ground black pepper

Preheat the oven to 400°F. Remove the papery skin from the garlic bulbs. Cut off ¼ inch from the stem ends. Place in an earthenware garlic baker or on a piece of foil. Drizzle with 1 teaspoon of olive oil. If using foil, wrap loosely around the garlic. Bake for 30-40 minutes, until the garlic cloves are soft. Remove from the oven and set aside.

While the garlic is baking, place the beets in a saucepan, cover with water, and bring to a boil. Boil for about 30 minutes, until the beets are tender. Drain and cut into ¼-inch thick slices. Toss in a little oil and place at one end of a large baking pan.

Slice the carrots and zucchini on the diagonal to make large slices, about ¼ inch thick. Transfer to the baking pan with the onion slices. Brush the vegetables with a little oil.

Roast the vegetables in the oven for about 10 minutes. Remove the zucchini if they are tender and golden. Continue to roast the remaining vegetables for 10-15 minutes more, until they are tender and golden. Roast a little longer if a charring effect is preferred. Remove from the oven and set aside.

Lightly toast all the bread slices. Squeeze the garlic cloves and spread the purée over four of the toasted slices. Arrange the roast vegetables over the four slices and top with the remaining toast. Serve at once while still warm. SERVES 4

CREAMY CHEESE SANDWICHES

Onion and Rosemary Bread (see page 12)
5 ounces mild, soft French goat cheese
3 plum tomatoes, sliced
Black Olive Paste (see page 14) or a
commercial variety
Salad leaves, to garnish

Cut 12 slices from the bread loaf. Spread half the slices with the goat cheese and top with slices of tomato.

Spread the remaining slices of bread with the Black Olive Paste and place on top of the tomatoes, paste sides down. Cut each sandwich in half. Serve three halves to each person, garnished with some green salad leaves. SERVES 4

RIGHT: Roast Vegetable Sandwich

HEARTY OPTIONS

The recipes in this chapter cater for those with hearty appetites, and many are influenced by the substantial sandwiches served in restaurants and delicatessens. Along with some variations on classic favorites from the deli, you will find more exotic alternatives, such as the hoisin-flavored Chinese Pork Rolls and the garlicky Greek Lamb Gyros. Some of the sandwiches can be a little messy to eat and are best served with a knife and fork, such as the Silver Dollars and the Mexican Sandwiches. Also featured are selections that make hearty breakfast sandwiches, such as Smoked Salmon & Egg Bagels.

SMOKED SALMON & EGG BAGELS

2 tablespoons butter
9 eggs
4 tablespoons milk
Salt and ground black pepper
1 cup roughly chopped smoked salmon
1 tablespoon chopped fresh parsley
4 bagels, split, lightly toasted and buttered
2 scallions, thinly sliced

Melt the butter in a nonstick skillet. Beat the eggs and milk together in a bowl, and season with salt and pepper. Pour the egg mixture into the skillet and cook over a medium heat, stirring to scramble the eggs.

When the eggs are almost set, stir in the smoked salmon and parsley. Cook for about 30 seconds more, until the eggs are cooked but still have a creamy appearance. Divide the scrambled eggs between the four bottom halves of the toasted bagels, garnish with the scallion, and cover with the tops of the bagels. Serve at once while still hot.   SERVES 4

OMELET SANDWICHES

3 tablespoons butter
1 small onion, finely chopped
1 pound fresh spinach, washed and roughly chopped, or 6 ounces frozen leaf spinach, thawed
Large pinch nutmeg
6 large eggs
Salt and ground black pepper
¾ cup grated cheddar cheese
2 slices whole-wheat or soft mixed-grain bread
Tomato wedges, to serve

Heat the butter in a 9-inch diameter nonstick skillet. Add the onion and cook for 4-5 minutes until golden. If using fresh spinach, place in a large saucepan with the water that remains on the leaves, and cook for 3-4 minutes until wilted, stirring all the time. Drain the excess liquid from the spinach. If using frozen spinach, press out excess water through a sieve. Stir the spinach into the onion and season with the nutmeg. Cook for 3-4 minutes to heat the spinach.

Beat the eggs and season with salt and pepper. Pour the eggs onto the spinach and scatter the cheese over the top. Reduce the heat to very low and cook for 8-10 minutes until almost set. Preheat a broiler to hot.

Place the skillet under the broiler and cook until the top of the omelet is set and golden.

To serve, cut the omelet into four wedges and place each portion between two slices of bread. Cut each sandwich in half and serve while still hot, accompanied by tomato wedges.   SERVES 4

RIGHT: Omelet Sandwich

THANKSGIVING TRIPLE-DECKER

For a very quick club sandwich, use turkey, stuffing and chunky cranberry sauce left-over from your Thanksgiving meal to make these sandwiches.

12 slices white bread
A little butter, softened
8 slices turkey

CRANBERRY SALSA

2 cups fresh cranberries
1 teaspoon chopped fresh ginger root
2 tablespoons sugar
3 scallions, finely chopped
2 tablespoons chopped fresh parsley

PORK STUFFING

8 ounces sausage meat
½ cup chopped bacon
½ cup finely chopped onion
½ cup breadcrumbs
1 tablespoon chopped fresh parsley
1 beaten egg
Ground black pepper

Prepare the salsa. Place the cranberries in a saucepan with the ginger and ¼ cup of water. Slowly bring to a boil and simmer until the cranberry skins burst. Stir in the sugar. Let the mixture cool. Add the scallion and parsley, and set aside. Use at room temperature.

To make the stuffing, preheat the oven to 350°F. Mix all the stuffing ingredients together in a bowl. Spoon the mixture into a 1-pound loaf pan, cover with foil, and bake for 40 minutes. Let cool before cutting into slices.

Toast the bread and butter each slice. To assemble each sandwich, place two slices of turkey on a slice of toast and spread over one-quarter of the Cranberry Salsa. Place another piece of toast on top and cover

with a slice of stuffing. Top with a third slice of toast and cut the sandwich into quarters. Repeat with the remaining ingredients to make three more clubs, and serve at once. SERVES 4

CHICKEN LICKIN' CLUBS

4 tablespoons mayonnaise
2 tablespoons shredded fresh basil leaves
Salt and ground black pepper
12 slices soft, mixed-grain white bread, toasted
Lollo biondo or crisp lettuce leaves
12 ounces cooked chicken breast, sliced
Extra virgin olive oil, to drizzle
8 slices prosciutto
1 large ripe pear

Mix the mayonnaise and basil in a bowl, and season with salt and pepper. Spread half the mayonnaise over four slices of toast. Top each with a layer of lettuce and divide the chicken slices between the sandwiches. Season with salt and pepper.

Spread four more slices of toast with the remaining mayonnaise and place on top of the chicken, mayonnaise sides down. Drizzle a little olive oil over the top of the toasted slices and arrange two slices of prosciutto on each sandwich. Slice the pear and layer slices on top of the prosciutto. Cover with the remaining slices of toast. Cut each sandwich into quarters and secure each with a wooden skewer before serving.

SERVES 4

CLOCKWISE: Thanksgiving Triple-Decker, Chicken Lickin' Club

PASTRAMI SANDWICHES WITH CARMELIZED ONIONS

8 slices Polish-style rye bread, buttered
Mild mustard
8 deli-style dill pickles, sliced
8 ounces sliced pastrami
Extra dill pickles, to serve (optional)

CARMELIZED ONIONS
I pound onions, thinly sliced
3 tablespoons olive oil
I tablespoon brown sugar
I tablespoon white wine vinegar
I tablespoon Worcestershire sauce

Prepare the Carmelized Onions. Place the onions and olive oil in a skillet and cook over a moderate heat for about 5 minutes, until the onions begin to soften. Stir in the brown sugar and continue to cook until the onions are soft and golden.

Add the vinegar, Worcestershire sauce and 3 tablespoons of water. Simmer until all the liquid has evaporated. Transfer the onions to a bowl and let cool.

Spread four of the slices of bread with mustard and divide the sliced dill pickles between them. Arrange the pastrami slices on top of each sandwich. Spoon one-quarter of the Carmelized Onions on top of each and cover with the remaining bread. Serve with extra dill pickles, if desired.   SERVES 4

REUBEN SANDWICHES

8 ounces sliced corned beef
8 slices light rye bread with caraway seeds, lightly buttered
I cup sauerkraut
4 tablespoons Thousand Island or Russian dressing
8 slices Swiss cheese
4 tablespoons butter
3 tablespoons olive oil
French fries, to serve (optional)

Arrange half the corned beef on four slices of the bread. Top each with one-quarter of the sauerkraut and I tablespoon Thousand Island or Russian dressing. Place two slices of Swiss cheese on each sandwich and finish with the remaining corned beef. Cover with the remaining slices of bread.

Heat half the butter with half the oil in a large skillet. Transfer two of the assembled sandwiches to the skillet. Place a plate or small chopping board on top of the sandwiches to press them down while they are cooking. Cook over a medium heat until golden and crisp. Turn over and cook the other side (by which time the cheese should have melted).

Repeat the cooking process for the two remaining sandwiches. Serve the reubens while still hot, with French fries, if desired.   SERVES 4

TOP: Reuben Sandwich
BOTTOM: Pastrami Sandwich with
Carmelized Onions

SILVER DOLLARS

4 small turkey breast fillets, about 1 pound
in total weight
1 tablespoon barbecue seasoning
2 tablespoons olive oil
4 large thick slices sourdough bread
12 slices bacon
2 cups julienne-cut zucchini
4 teaspoons sesame seeds
Boiled baby new potatoes, to serve (optional)

WELSH RAREBIT

2 tablespoons butter
1 tablespoon flour
3 tablespoons milk
2 tablespoons beer
1 cup grated cheddar cheese
1 teaspoon Dijon mustard
1 teaspoon Worcestershire sauce

Preheat a broiler to hot. Place the turkey fillets between plastic wrap and pound with a wooden meat pounder until no more than ½ inch thick. Sprinkle over the barbecue seasoning and brush with a little of the olive oil.

Place the turkey fillets on a broiler rack and cook under the broiler for about 15 minutes until tender, turning once. Toast the bread under the broiler during this time.

Meanwhile, heat the remaining oil in a large skillet. Add the bacon and fry on both sides until crisp and golden. While the bacon is cooking, prepare the Welsh Rarebit.

Melt the butter in a saucepan. Add the flour and cook over a low heat for 2 minutes, stirring constantly. Add the milk and beer, and stir until the mixture is smooth and thick. Add the cheese, mustard and Worcestershire sauce and stir until the cheese has melted. Remove from the heat and set aside.

Lift the cooked bacon from the skillet and drain on paper towels.

Place the zucchini strips in the skillet and sauté until golden and tender. Set aside.

Remove the turkey from the broiler. Spread the Welsh Rarebit over the four slices of toast and place under the broiler until bubbling.

To assemble, arrange three slices of bacon on top of each sandwich and top each with a turkey breast. Pile one-quarter of the zucchini on top of each and sprinkle 1 teaspoon of sesame seeds over each sandwich. Serve at once while still hot, accompanied by the new potatoes if desired. SERVES 4

BACON, LETTUCE & TOMATO SANDWICHES

8 thick slices bacon
8 thick slices white bread
Mayonnaise
4 tomatoes, sliced
Lettuce leaves

Preheat a broiler to hot. Place the bacon on a broiler rack and cook under the broiler until crisp and golden. Meanwhile toast the bread and spread each slice with a generous helping of mayonnaise. Arrange tomato slices on four slices of toast. Top each with some lettuce leaves and two slices of bacon. Cover each sandwich with the remaining toast, cut in half, and serve at once. SERVES 4

Variation: Spread the top slices of toast with crunchy peanut butter for an interesting alternative.

RIGHT: Silver Dollar

MEDITERRANEAN CHICKEN SANDWICHES

These sandwiches can be served either hot or cold, depending on your preference.

4 small, skinless, boneless chicken breasts
2 cloves garlic, crushed
2 tablespoons olive oil
1 teaspoon dried Mediterranean herbs
Salt and ground black pepper
3 tablespoons plain or garlic mayonnaise
8 slices sun-dried tomato bread
2 large plum tomatoes, sliced
Handful of fresh basil leaves
Red and yellow cherry tomato salad, to serve (optional)

Carefully cut the chicken breasts in half horizontally to make eight thin slices. Transfer to a shallow glass or ceramic dish.

Mix the garlic, olive oil, herbs, and salt and pepper together in a small bowl. Pour over the chicken, tossing to coat well. Cover with plastic wrap and let marinate for 1 hour.

Heat a nonstick skillet or ridged griddle pan. Transfer the chicken slices from the dish to the pan and cook over a moderately high heat for 2-3 minutes on each side, until golden. Remove from the heat. If serving the sandwiches cold, transfer the chicken to a plate and set aside to cool.

Spread the mayonnaise on four slices of bread. Arrange tomato slices on the bread and top each slice with two pieces of chicken. Season with salt and pepper, and scatter a few basil leaves on top. Cover with the remaining bread and serve hot or cold, accompanied by the tomato salad if desired. SERVES 4

STEAK SANDWICHES WITH RED ONION RELISH

4 very thin sandwich steaks
Steak seasoning
2 tablespoons olive oil
8 slices crusty white bread, lightly toasted
French fries, to serve (optional)

RED ONION RELISH
2 tablespoons olive oil
2 cups sliced red onions
1 tablespoon brown sugar
2 tablespoons red wine vinegar
Small dollop of butter

Prepare the relish. Heat the olive oil in a skillet. Add the onions and cook gently for 15-20 minutes, until the onions are tender. Pour in ⅔ cup water, add the brown sugar and vinegar, and simmer until almost all the liquid has evaporated and the onions are tender. Stir in the butter and set aside (this relish is best served while warm).

Season the steaks with a little steak seasoning. Heat a ridged griddle pan or large skillet and pour in the olive oil. Cook the steaks over a high heat for 2-3 minutes on each side. Place a cooked steak on each of four toasted bread slices. Top with the relish and cover with the remaining toasted bread. Serve at once while still hot, accompanied by French fries if desired. SERVES 4

Variation: To make a Cheese Steak Sandwich, top each steak with a thin slice of cheese and melt the cheese under a hot broiler before topping the sandwich with the relish. You may like to use a hoagie roll in place of the white bread.

TOP: Steak Sandwich with Red Onion Relish
BOTTOM: Mediterranean Chicken Sandwich

HOT ITALIAN HOAGIES WITH POTATO WEDGES

4 whole-wheat hoagie rolls
3 tomatoes, skinned and sliced (see Tomato and
Herb Salsa on page 14 for skinning tomatoes)
Salt and ground black pepper
4 ounces sliced cold meat, such as ham,
salami or mortadella
6 ounces Dolcelatte cheese

POTATO WEDGES

2 large baking potatoes
3 tablespoons olive oil
Salt

Preheat the oven to 400°F. Prepare the potatoes. Scrub the potatoes and cut into 12 thin wedges. Place in a roasting pan, pour over the olive oil, and toss until the wedges are well coated with oil. Season with a little salt. Bake for 40 minutes, turning once during cooking, until the potato wedges are crisp and golden.

Meanwhile split the hoagie rolls in half lengthwise. Place a layer of tomatoes on the bottom of each roll and season with salt and pepper.

Cut the sliced meat in half and divide between the rolls, arranging the slices in overlapping folds.

Cut the cheese into rough slices (the cheese is soft so the slices will be irregular shapes) and add to the sandwiches. Place the bread lids on top and wrap each sandwich in foil. Place in the oven during the last 15 minutes of the cooking time for the Potato Wedges. Unwrap the hoagies and serve hot, accompanied by the crisp Potato Wedges.   SERVES 4

HOT SALAMI BAGUETTES

1 medium French baguette, about 16 inches long
2 tablespoons olive oil
2 medium onions, thinly sliced
4 cloves garlic, thinly sliced
2 red bell peppers, cored, seeded and thinly sliced
6 tomatoes, skinned and chopped (See Tomato and
Herb Salsa on page 14 for skinning tomatoes)
Pinch of hot chili flakes
Salt and ground black pepper
8 ounces Milano salami
1½ cups roughly chopped mozzarella cheese
1 teaspoon dried oregano
Crisp green salad, to serve (optional)

Cut the baguette in half and then each piece in half lengthwise to produce four portions.

Heat the olive oil in a skillet. Add the onions and cook for 4-5 minutes until lightly browned. Add the garlic and bell peppers, and cook for about 2 minutes. Stir in the tomatoes and chili flakes, and cook for about 3 minutes more, until the tomatoes begin to soften. Season the mixture with salt and pepper. Preheat a broiler to hot.

Spoon one-quarter of the tomato mixture onto each portion of baguette. Divide the salami between each, folding over the slices so they fit onto the bread. Scatter the chopped mozzarella cheese on top and sprinkle on the oregano.

Place the open-face baguettes under the broiler and cook until the cheese melts. Serve while still hot, accompanied by a crisp green salad if desired.
          SERVES 4

TOP: Hot Salami Baguette
BOTTOM: Hot Italian Hoagie with
Potato Wedges

MEATBALL SANDWICHES

3 tablespoons olive oil
I cup beef stock
2 tablespoons butter
I large onion, sliced
4 thick slices country-style white bread, toasted

MEATBALLS

I pound lean ground beef
½ cup finely chopped onion
½ cup whole-wheat breadcrumbs
½ teaspoon paprika
¼ teaspoon allspice
¼ teaspoon grated nutmeg
I beaten egg
Salt and ground black pepper

THREE-MUSTARD MAYONNAISE

4 tablespoons mayonnaise
I tablespoon grainy mustard
I teaspoon English mustard
I teaspoon Dijon mustard
I teaspoon honey

Place all the ingredients for the meatballs into a food processor. Mix together by operating the processor in short bursts. Form into about 36 small balls.

Mix all the ingredients for the Three-Mustard Mayonnaise together in a bowl. Set aside.

Heat 2 tablespoons of the olive oil in a large skillet. Add the meatballs and fry until they are browned all over. Pour in the stock and simmer for 15 minutes, or until three-quarters of the liquid has evaporated.

Meanwhile, heat the remaining oil and butter in a separate skillet, and cook the onions until crispy.

To serve, spread all the toasted bread with the mustard mayonnaise. Pile one-quarter of the meatballs on each slice and top each with one-quarter of the crispy onions. Serve hot.   SERVES 4

MEATLOAF SANDWICHES

Meatloaf sandwiches are delicious when served hot, but can also be eaten cold if you prefer.

2 tablespoons olive oil
I medium onion, chopped
I clove garlic
1½ cups chopped mushrooms
I pound lean ground beef
¾ cup fresh breadcrumbs
2 tablespoons chopped fresh parsley
I tablespoon Worcestershire sauce
I beaten egg
½ teaspoon dried thyme
Few drops Tabasco
Pinch of allspice
Salt and ground pepper
8-12 slices chollah or country-style white bread, lightly buttered
Mustard or ketchup (optional)
Corn Relish, to serve (see page 14)

Preheat the oven to 350°F. Heat the olive oil in a skillet. Add the onion and cook gently until soft. Add the garlic and mushrooms, and cook until the mushrooms are just tender. Transfer to a large mixing bowl.

Add the ground beef, breadcrumbs, parsley, Worcestershire sauce, egg, thyme, Tabasco and allspice to the mixture. Season and mix together well. Transfer to a 2-pound loaf pan. Cover with foil and bake for about I hour. Let cool slightly in the pan.

To serve, turn the meatloaf out of the pan and slice. Place each slice between slices of buttered bread, adding mustard or ketchup if desired. Serve accompanied by the Corn Relish.   SERVES 4-6

RIGHT: Meatball Sandwich

CHINESE PORK ROLLS

1½-pound piece pork fillet
1 small red bell pepper, cored, seeded and thinly sliced
4 scallions, thinly sliced
12 canned water chestnuts, drained and sliced
1 cup shredded Chinese cabbage
2 teaspoons sunflower or sesame oil
2 teaspoons dark soy sauce
4 large, soft, white buns, split
Scallion tassels, to garnish

MARINADE

2 tablespoons dark soy sauce
1 tablespoon dry sherry
1 tablespoon hoisin sauce
2 teaspoons sunflower oil
2 cloves garlic, crushed
2 teaspoons honey
1 tablespoon chopped fresh ginger root
½ teaspoon Chinese five-spice powder

Place the pork in a shallow glass or ceramic dish. Mix the marinade ingredients together in a small bowl and pour over the pork. Cover and marinate for at least 2 hours or, preferably, overnight in the refrigerator.

Preheat the oven to 400°F. Lift the pork from the marinade and place on a wire rack in a roasting pan. Cook for about 30 minutes until tender, basting occasionally with the remaining marinade. Set aside.

Mix the red bell pepper, scallion, water chestnuts and Chinese cabbage together in a bowl. Pour the oil and soy sauce over and toss together to combine.

Slice the pork and divide between the split buns. Top each with one-quarter of the vegetable mixture and serve garnished with scallion tassels.   SERVES 4

MEXICAN SANDWICHES

1 pound stir-fry pork or pork fillet, cut into thin strips
2 teaspoons ground cumin
1 teaspoon mild chili powder
½ teaspoon ground coriander
½ teaspoon salt
½ teaspoon ground black pepper
3 tablespoons sunflower oil
Cornmeal Bread (see page 10)
1 avocado, peeled, pitted and sliced
Tomato and Herb Salsa (see page 14)
¾ cup grated cheddar cheese
Pickled hot chilies, to garnish
Green salad, to serve

Place the pork in a shallow glass dish. Mix the cumin, chili, coriander, salt and pepper together in a small bowl. Scatter the mixed seasoning over the pork, tossing to coat evenly. Set the pork aside for at least 30 minutes.

Heat the sunflower oil in a large skillet or wok. Add the pork and stir-fry for 8-10 minutes, until cooked.

Cut the Cornmeal Bread into four squares and cut each square in half horizontally.

Arrange avocado slices on the base of each cornmeal square. Divide the pork between the portions. Spoon the Tomato and Herb Salsa on the sandwiches, and finish with the grated cheese. Place a bread lid on each sandwich. Serve immediately, garnished with pickled chilies and accompanied by a green salad.

SERVES 4

TOP: Mexican Sandwich
BOTTOM: Chinese Pork Roll

TANDOORI CHICKEN PITAS

4 small, skinless, boneless chicken breasts
½ cup long-grain or basmati rice
½ cup chopped, ready-to-eat, dried apricots
4-inch piece cucumber, diced
1 tablespoon mayonnaise
3 tablespoons plain yogurt
4 individual pita breads
Green salad, to serve

TANDOORI MARINADE
⅔ cup plain yogurt
2 tablespoons lemon juice
1 tablespoon ground coriander
2 teaspoons mild curry paste
¼ teaspoon chili powder

Place the chicken in a shallow glass dish. Mix all the Tandoori Marinade ingredients together in a bowl. Spoon the marinade over the chicken to coat well. Cover with plastic wrap and refrigerate for at least 2 hours, but preferably overnight.

Preheat a broiler to medium-hot. Place the chicken in a broiler pan and cook under the broiler for 15-20 minutes, turning once, until the chicken is tender. Remove and set aside. When cooled, dice the chicken.

While the chicken is cooking, boil the rice until tender, according to the instructions on the package. Drain the rice, rinse under cold water, and drain again.

Place the cooked rice in a bowl with the apricots, cucumber and diced chicken. Mix the mayonnaise with the yogurt and stir into the chicken mixture.

Split the pitas to make pockets and spoon one-quarter of the tandoori chicken into each one. Serve the pitas with the green salad.   SERVES 4

GREEK LAMB GYROS

1½-pound fillet-end leg of lamb
4 Greek bread rolls or pita breads
Romaine lettuce leaves
Handful of fresh mint leaves, shredded
Red Pepper Relish (see page 14)
Black olives, to serve

MARINADE
3 tablespoons olive oil
1 tablespoon tomato paste
3 cloves garlic, finely chopped
1 teaspoon dried Mediterranean herbs
Grated zest and juice of 1 lemon
Salt and ground black pepper

Using a sharp knife, remove the bones from the joint of lamb, but leave the meat in one long piece.

Mix the marinade ingredients together in a bowl. Spread the marinade all over the lamb, coating well. Place the joint in a roasting pan and set aside for about 1 hour. Preheat the oven to 400°F.

Cook the lamb for about 45 minutes, until tender and slightly pink in the middle. Transfer to a board, cover with foil, and leave for 10 minutes before slicing.

Split the bread rolls. Divide the lettuce leaves and mint between the bottom halves of the bread and top with slices of lamb. Spoon one-quarter of the Red Pepper Relish over each and top with the bread lids. Serve immediately, accompanied by olives.   SERVES 4

Variation: Spread the garlic purée from a bulb of roasted garlic (see Roast Vegetable Sandwiches on page 44) on the bottom halves of the sandwiches for an extra garlicky flavor.

TOP: Greek Lamb Gyro
BOTTOM: Tandoori Chicken Pitas

SPICY FISHWICHES

½ cup long-grain rice
1 pound fresh cod or haddock fillet
4 scallions, chopped
20 cashews
2 small fresh red chilies, seeded and chopped
2 teaspoons light soy sauce
1 small beaten egg
Oil for frying
8 large slices white or brown bread, buttered

CILANTRO SALSA
1½ cups fresh cilantro leaves
2 cloves garlic, chopped
1-2 fresh green chilies, seeded and chopped
1 green bell pepper, cored, seeded and chopped
2 teaspoons finely chopped fresh ginger root
2 tablespoons plain yogurt

Boil the rice until tender, according to the instructions on the package. Rinse the rice under cold water and drain well. Set aside.

Skin the fish, remove any bones, and chop the flesh roughly. Transfer to a food processor and add the scallions, cashews and chili. Blend until all the ingredients are chopped.

Add the soy sauce, egg and rice, and blend briefly to mix (do not let the mixture become a paste). Transfer to a bowl and refrigerate for about 1 hour.

Meanwhile, make the salsa. Place the cilantro, garlic, chilies, bell pepper and ginger into the bowl of the food processor. Blend until finely chopped. Transfer to a mixing bowl and stir in the yogurt. Refrigerate until required.

Shape the fish mixture into 16 small flat patties. Pour enough oil into a skillet to cover the bottom. Heat the oil and cook the fish cakes over a medium heat for 3-4 minutes on each side until golden. Drain on paper towels.

To serve, place four fish cakes on each of four slices of buttered bread. Place a spoonful of Cilantro Salsa on each sandwich, and cover with the remaining four slices of bread. Cut each sandwich in half and serve while still warm.   SERVES 4

SHRIMP ROLLS WITH AVOCADO SALSA

4 long, soft hoagie or hot-dog rolls
8 ounces peeled, cooked shrimp
1 teaspoon grated lemon zest
Lettuce leaves and lemon wedges, to garnish

AVOCADO SALSA
1 medium avocado
2 tablespoons lemon or lime juice
2 tomatoes, finely diced
4 scallions, finely chopped
1 tablespoon olive oil
1 tablespoon chopped fresh parsley
Salt and ground black pepper

Prepare the salsa. Halve the avocado, remove the pit, and peel. Dice the flesh. Place the avocado in a bowl with the lemon or lime juice and gently toss together. Add the remaining salsa ingredients, seasoning with salt and pepper.

Split the rolls lengthwise, but keep them intact. Spoon one-quarter of the salsa into each roll. Mix the shrimp with the lemon zest and carefully divide between the rolls. Serve garnished with lettuce leaves and lemon wedges.   SERVES 4

RIGHT: Spicy Fishwich

SANDWICHES TO GO

Because sandwiches are the most popular food to transport, this chapter is devoted to a range of flavorful filled rolls and sandwiches that are suitable for packed lunches and picnics. There are special stuffed loafs, such as the Mediterranean Picnic Loaf, which are whole loaves of bread filled with layers of ingredients. These giant sandwiches are ideal for picnics because they can be transported whole and cut into thick slices or wedges when required. When packing sandwiches, it is a good idea to refrigerate them before wrapping securely in plastic wrap or wax paper.

FILLED POPPYSEED ROLLS

4 poppyseed bread rolls
I red apple
I tablespoon lemon juice
2 stalks celery, chopped
½ cup crumbled Lancashire or Cheshire cheese
¼ cup chopped walnuts
2 tablespoons sour cream
2 tablespoons mayonnaise

Cut the top off each poppyseed roll and reserve for using as a lid. Using a serrated-edged knife, scoop out the soft insides.

Core and chop the apple into small pieces, place in a small bowl, and toss with the lemon juice. Add the celery, crumbled cheese and walnuts.

Stir the sour cream and mayonnaise together in a separate bowl, then fold the dressing into the salad ingredients. Spoon the filling into the scooped-out rolls, pressing down firmly. Replace the bread lids. Wrap before packing into a lunchbox or picnic basket.

SERVES 4

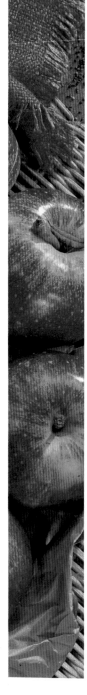

BRIE & ROAST PEPPER ROLLS

2 red bell peppers
2 tablespoons extra virgin olive oil
2 cloves garlic, thinly sliced
4 country-style bread rolls
8 sun-dried tomatoes in oil
6 ounces ripe Brie
Fresh basil leaves

Preheat a broiler to hot. Place the bell peppers under the broiler and turn until the skin is charred all over. Remove the peppers and place them in a plastic bag. Set aside for 20 minutes. Peel off the skin, discard the seeds, and cut the flesh into strips.

Place the strips in a bowl, pour the olive oil over the top, and toss together with the sliced garlic. Set aside.

Cut the rolls in half horizontally. Place two sun-dried tomatoes on the bottom half of each roll with a little drizzle of the oil they are packed in. Slice the Brie and arrange on top of each sandwich.

Spoon over the roasted peppers with the garlic, scatter a few basil leaves on top, and replace the lids. Wrap and refrigerate until required.   SERVES 4

Variation: Substitute buffalo mozzarella for the Brie in the recipe.

LEFT: Filled Poppyseed Rolls
RIGHT: Brie & Roast Pepper Roll

CORNED BEEF SURPRISE

4 large whole-wheat buns
A little butter, softened
Lettuce leaves
4 thick slices canned corned beef

SPICED APPLE RELISH

1 tablespoon oil
2 small onions, chopped
1 teaspoon ground cumin
1 teaspoon ground coriander
1/4 teaspoon cinnamon
Large pinch of nutmeg
2 cups chopped Granny Smith apples
2/3 cup water
1 tablespoon lemon juice

To make the relish, heat the oil in a medium-sized saucepan. Add the onion and cook gently for 3 minutes, until the onions begin to soften.

Stir in the spices and then the chopped apple, water and lemon juice. Simmer uncovered for 10-15 minutes, stirring until the mixture becomes soft and most of the liquid has evaporated. Transfer the relish to a bowl and let cool.

Split the bread buns. Lightly butter the cut sides and place a layer of lettuce on each base. Add a slice of corned beef to each and top with a generous layer of Spiced Apple Relish. Cover with the bread lids, cut each sandwich in half, and, if desired, wrap for a lunchbox or picnic.   SERVES 4

FARMHOUSE SANDWICHES

Small bag of prepared salad leaves
1 tablespoon walnut oil
1 tablespoon extra virgin olive oil
2 teaspoons red wine vinegar
Salt and ground black pepper
8 ounces mature Stilton cheese, crumbled
8 slices crusty white bread, lightly buttered
1/2 cup walnut pieces

Place the salad leaves in a bowl. Whisk together the oils and vinegar, and season with salt and pepper. Pour the dressing over the leaves and toss together.

Divide the cheese between four slices of bread. Press down gently, top with the salad, and scatter the walnut pieces over the top. Cover with the remaining bread. Wrap and pack in a lunchbox or picnic basket, if desired.   SERVES 4

Variation: You may like to use another variety of crumbly cheese, such as Caerphilly or Wensleydale, or even cheddar or Colby in place of the Stilton.

RIGHT: Farmhouse Sandwich

PROVENCAL HAM ROLLS

4 ciabatta or crusty white bread rolls
6 ounces thinly sliced ham
2 large tomatoes, sliced (optional)
Fresh basil leaves (optional)

EGGPLANT SPREAD

1 eggplant, about 10 ounces in weight
Olive oil, to brush
1 red bell pepper
1 cup pitted kalamata olives
1 clove garlic, crushed
2 teaspoons lemon juice
6 fresh basil leaves
1 tablespoon olive oil
Salt and ground black pepper

Preheat the oven to 400°F. Make the spread. Halve the eggplant and prick the skin all over. Brush the eggplant with the oil and place in a large roasting pan, cut sides down.

Halve the red bell pepper, core, and remove the seeds. Brush with oil and place in the roasting pan with the eggplant. Bake the vegetables for about 30 minutes, until tender.

Scoop the flesh from the eggplant and squeeze out the excess liquid. Place the flesh in a food processor. Peel the skin from the bell pepper and roughly chop the flesh. Add to the processor with the olives, garlic, lemon juice, basil and olive oil. Blend until finely chopped. Season to taste with salt and pepper.

Cut the rolls in half horizontally and spread the bottom halves generously with the Eggplant Spread. Arrange the ham on top of each sandwich. Divide the tomato between the rolls and add a basil leaf, if desired. Place the bread lids on top. Wrap and refrigerate before packing for a lunchbox or picnic.

SERVES 4

ITALIAN SANDWICH SLICES

1 flat country-style bread loaf, such as ciabatta
Extra virgin olive oil
Handful of salad leaves, such as radicchio, curly endive and escarole
4 ounces sliced garlic sausage or Italian salami
Olives, to serve (optional)

TOMATO SALAD

4 firm ripe tomatoes, chopped
1 small red onion, finely chopped
1 tablespoon chopped fresh basil or parsley
1 teaspoon balsamic vinegar
Salt and ground black pepper

Prepare the Tomato Salad. Place the chopped tomatoes in a bowl with the onion, herbs and vinegar. Season well with salt and pepper and mix together to combine. Set aside.

Cut the bread in half lengthwise and moisten the cut surface with olive oil. Place a layer of salad leaves on the base, add the sliced garlic sausage or salami, then carefully spoon over the Tomato Salad.

Cover with the bread top and gently press the sandwich together. Wrap tightly in plastic wrap and refrigerate before packing for a picnic. To serve, cut the loaf into four portions and serve with with the olives, if desired. SERVES 4

Variation: Omit the garlic sausage and use 6 ounces of mozzarella cheese (preferably the buffalo variety), sliced. Add some thick slices of roast yellow bell pepper (see Brie and Roast Pepper Rolls on page 66 for roasting peppers).

TOP: Italian Sandwich Slices
BOTTOM: Provençal Ham Roll

ROAST BEEF SANDWICHES WITH GARLIC BUTTER

I large whole bulb garlic

I teaspoon olive oil

4 tablespoons butter, softened

4 tablespoons crème fraîche or mayonnaise

2 tablespoons horseradish sauce

8 slices soft mixed-grain bread

10 ounces rare roast beef, thinly sliced

½ Spanish onion, thinly sliced

To roast the garlic, preheat the oven to 400°F. Remove the papery skin from the bulb of garlic. Cut off ¼ inch from the stem end. Place in an earthenware garlic baker or on a piece of foil and drizzle over the olive oil. If using foil, wrap loosely. Bake for 40 minutes, until the cloves are soft. Let cool.

Squeeze the garlic to remove it from the skin and beat into the butter to combine. Mix the crème fraîche or mayonnaise and horseradish sauce in a separate mixing bowl. Set aside.

Spread the garlic butter over four slices of bread. Divide the slices of roast beef between them. Top with onion slices and finish each with a dollop of the horseradish mixture. Cover with the remaining bread and cut each sandwich in half. Wrap for a lunchbox or picnic, if desired. SERVES 4

TURKEY SANDWICHES WITH CONFETTI SLAW

8 slices light rye bread

A little butter or polyunsaturated margarine, softened

Crisp lettuce leaves

8 ounces wafer-thin turkey

CONFETTI SLAW

I cup finely shredded red cabbage

I cup finely shredded white cabbage

½ cup finely shredded broccoli stalks

I small carrot, peeled and grated

2 tablespoons reduced-calorie mayonnaise

2 tablespoons plain yogurt

Salt and ground black pepper

Begin by making the slaw. Place the prepared vegetables in a bowl. In a separate bowl, mix together the mayonnaise and yogurt, and season well. Stir the dressing into the vegetables and toss gently to coat. Set aside.

Lightly butter the slices of bread. Cover four slices with crisp lettuce leaves and divide the turkey between them. Top with the Confetti Slaw, cover with the remaining slices of rye bread, and gently press together. Wrap in foil or plastic wrap and refrigerate before packing in a lunchbox or for a picnic.

SERVES 4

RIGHT: Turkey Sandwiches with Confetti Slaw

SEAFOOD SUBS

7-ounce can tuna in water, drained
4 ounces peeled, cooked shrimp
4 individual hoagie rolls or baguettes
A little butter, softened
½ cup shredded lettuce
16 slices cucumber

SUN-DRIED TOMATO AIOLI

1 large clove garlic
¼ teaspoon salt
4 tablespoons mayonnaise
5 oil-packed sun-dried tomatoes, drained

Prepare the aïoli. Place the garlic in a bowl with the salt and mash with the back of a spoon until crushed. Beat in the mayonnaise. Finely chop the sun-dried tomatoes and add them to the mayonnaise. Stir until well blended.

Flake the tuna. Fold the tuna into the tomato aïoli with the shrimp.

Cut the hoagie rolls or baguettes in half lengthwise and butter the bottom half of each. Top with a layer of shredded lettuce and cucumber slices, then spoon over the shrimp and tuna filling. Cover with the top halves of the bread. Wrap in foil or plastic wrap, and refrigerate until required.   SERVES 4

GIANT VEGETARIAN HERO

1 long crusty French bread loaf or giant hoagie roll
2 cloves garlic, halved
Extra virgin olive oil
3 ripe tomatoes, sliced
½ small head Florence fennel, thinly sliced
1 small red or yellow bell pepper, cored, seeded and thinly sliced
½ small red onion, thinly sliced
8 black olives, pitted and halved
Handful of shredded fresh basil leaves
Salt and ground black pepper
Extra black olives, to serve (optional)

Cut the loaf lengthwise. Remove a little of the soft middle. Rub the inside of the bread with the cut sides of the garlic, and generously drizzle with olive oil.

Layer the slices of tomato, fennel, bell pepper and onion on the bottom half of the loaf. Top with the olives and basil. Season with salt and pepper, and drizzle with a little extra olive oil. Cover with the top of the loaf. Wrap in plastic wrap and place a weight on top of the loaf for 30 minutes.

If the loaf is for a picnic, refrigerate until ready to pack. To serve, unwrap and cut into four portions. Serve accompanied by extra olives, if desired.

SERVES 4

LEFT: Seafood Subs
RIGHT: Giant Vegetarian Hero

ROAST EGGPLANT & TOMATO SANDWICHES

The eggplant and tomatoes can be prepared the day before and stored in an airtight container in the refrigerator until required.

2 small eggplants, about 12 ounces in weight
Salt
3 tablespoons olive oil
1 teaspoon ground cumin
6 large tomatoes, skinned (see Tomato and Herb Salsa on page 14 for skinning tomatoes)
3 cloves garlic, finely chopped
Extra olive oil, to drizzle
Ground black pepper
1 tablespoon chopped fresh oregano or ½ teaspoon dried oregano
8 slices country-style white bread
5 tablespoons pine nuts, lightly toasted

Cut the eggplant into ¼-inch thick slices. Sprinkle with salt and leave to drain in a colander for 30 minutes. Preheat a broiler to hot. Rinse the eggplant slices and pat them dry with paper towels. Place in a broiler pan.

Mix together the oil and cumin, then brush the eggplant with half the oil. Broil the eggplant until golden, turn the slices over, brush with the remaining oil, and cook again until golden. Transfer the eggplant to a plate and let cool.

Preheat the oven to 400°F. Cut each tomato into three slices, and place in a roasting pan. Scatter over the garlic, drizzle with a little olive oil, season with black pepper, and sprinkle with the oregano. Cook for 30 minutes, until the tomatoes are slightly charred. Let cool.

Arrange the eggplant slices on four slices of bread. Top with the tomatoes, scatter over the pine nuts, and finish with the remaining bread.　　SERVES 4

MEDITERRANEAN PICNIC LOAF

1 small, traditional, crusty bread loaf
3 tablespoons pesto sauce
8 ounces cooked, skinned chicken breast
2 cups shredded arugula or young spinach leaves
3 plum tomatoes, sliced
2 tablespoons olive oil
Salt and ground black pepper
5 ounces mozzarella cheese, sliced
4 ounces antipasto artichokes in oil, drained
4 ounces sliced, cooked tongue
A little butter, softened

Cut off the base of the loaf, about ½ inch from the bottom. Scoop out the inside from the top of the loaf so the walls are also ½ inch thick.

Spread the pesto around the inside of the hollowed-out loaf. Cut the chicken into thick slices and place half of them inside the loaf. Add a layer of half the arugula or spinach, then a layer of tomatoes, using half the amount. Drizzle over half the olive oil.

Season with salt and pepper, then add all of the cheese and the artichokes. Add the remaining tomatoes and season again. Top with all the tongue and the remaining chicken. Finally add the remaining arugula or spinach, drizzle over the remaining oil, and season.

Butter the edge of the base and place on the loaf. Wrap tightly in plastic wrap and refrigerate overnight. To serve, unwrap and slice.　　SERVES 4-6

Variation: Substitute Black Olive Paste (see page 14) for the pesto in the recipe. Use salami and Fontina cheese in place of the chicken, tongue and mozzarella. A round country loaf can be substituted for the traditional loaf, if preferred.

RIGHT: Mediterranean Picnic Loaf

SALAMI & HERB CHEESE WEDGES

Any flavor of Italian focaccia bread can be used in this recipe. Onion, cheese, garlic and herb, and sun-dried tomato varieties, all make interesting sandwiches.

2 tablespoons extra virgin olive oil
I small onion, sliced
I small red bell pepper, cored, seeded and sliced
I small yellow bell pepper, cored, seeded and sliced
I focaccia bread, about 10 ounces in weight
3 ounces soft herb cheese, such as
Boursin aux fines herbes
15 slices cucumber
Lettuce leaves
Salt and ground black pepper
4 ounces thinly sliced salami

Heat the olive oil in a skillet. Add the onion and cook for 3-4 minutes, until the onion begins to soften. Add the sliced bell peppers and continue to cook until the peppers are tender, stirring constantly. Transfer to a plate and set aside to cool.

Cut the focaccia bread in half horizontally. Spread the soft herb cheese on the base and arrange the cucumber slices on top. Add a few lettuce leaves and season with salt and pepper.

Layer the salami over the lettuce and top with the prepared pepper mixture. Cover with the top of the focaccia. Wrap in foil or plastic wrap and refrigerate until required. To serve, cut the loaf into wedges.

SERVES 4

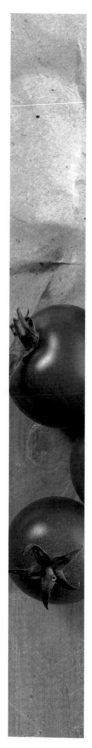

CHEESE & HAM WEDGES

I large, round country-style bread loaf
A little butter, softened
4 ounces cheddar or Swiss cheese, thinly sliced
4 tablespoons spicy fruit chutney, such as
peach chutney
6 ounces sliced honey-roast ham
½ bunch watercress, washed and trimmed
Cherry tomatoes, to serve (optional)

Cut the loaf in half horizontally. Remove a little of the crumb from the top half, then spread butter on both sides of the loaf.

Arrange the slices of cheese on the base, and spread the chutney evenly over the cheese. Arrange the ham on top, overlapping each slice. Cover the ham with the watercress and place the bread lid on top. Press the loaf together gently. Wrap in foil or plastic wrap, and refrigerate until required. To serve, cut into wedges and serve with cherry tomatoes, if desired.

SERVES 4-6

TOP LEFT: Salami & Herb Cheese Wedges
BOTTOM RIGHT: Cheese & Ham Wedges

INDEX